I0485635

Adult Coloring Book
Roses

Relax with this Calming, Stress Managment, Floral Adult Coloring Book of Roses

Grahame David Garlick

www.southshorepublications.com

ISBN-13: 978-1518778582
ISBN-10: 1518778585

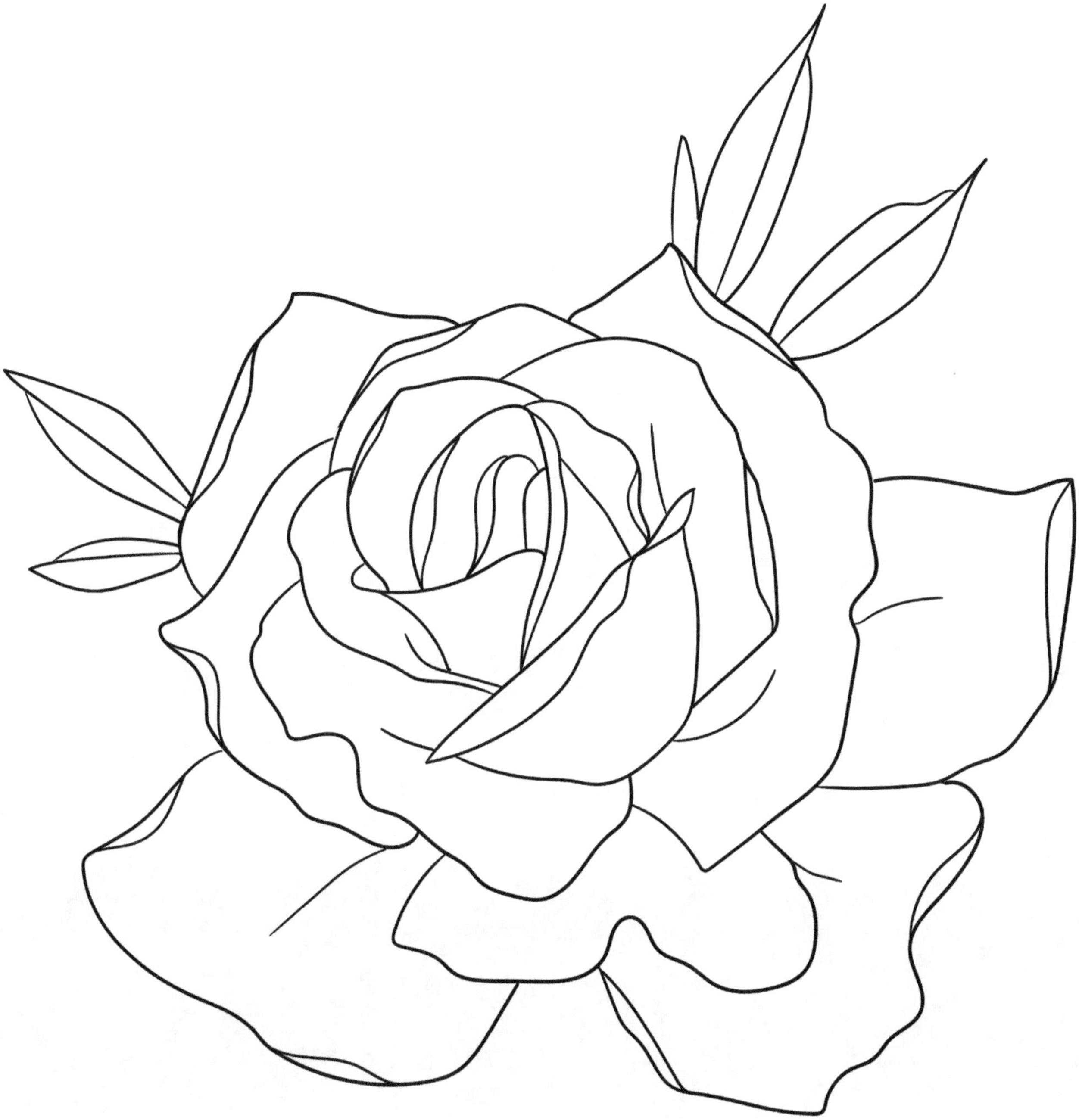

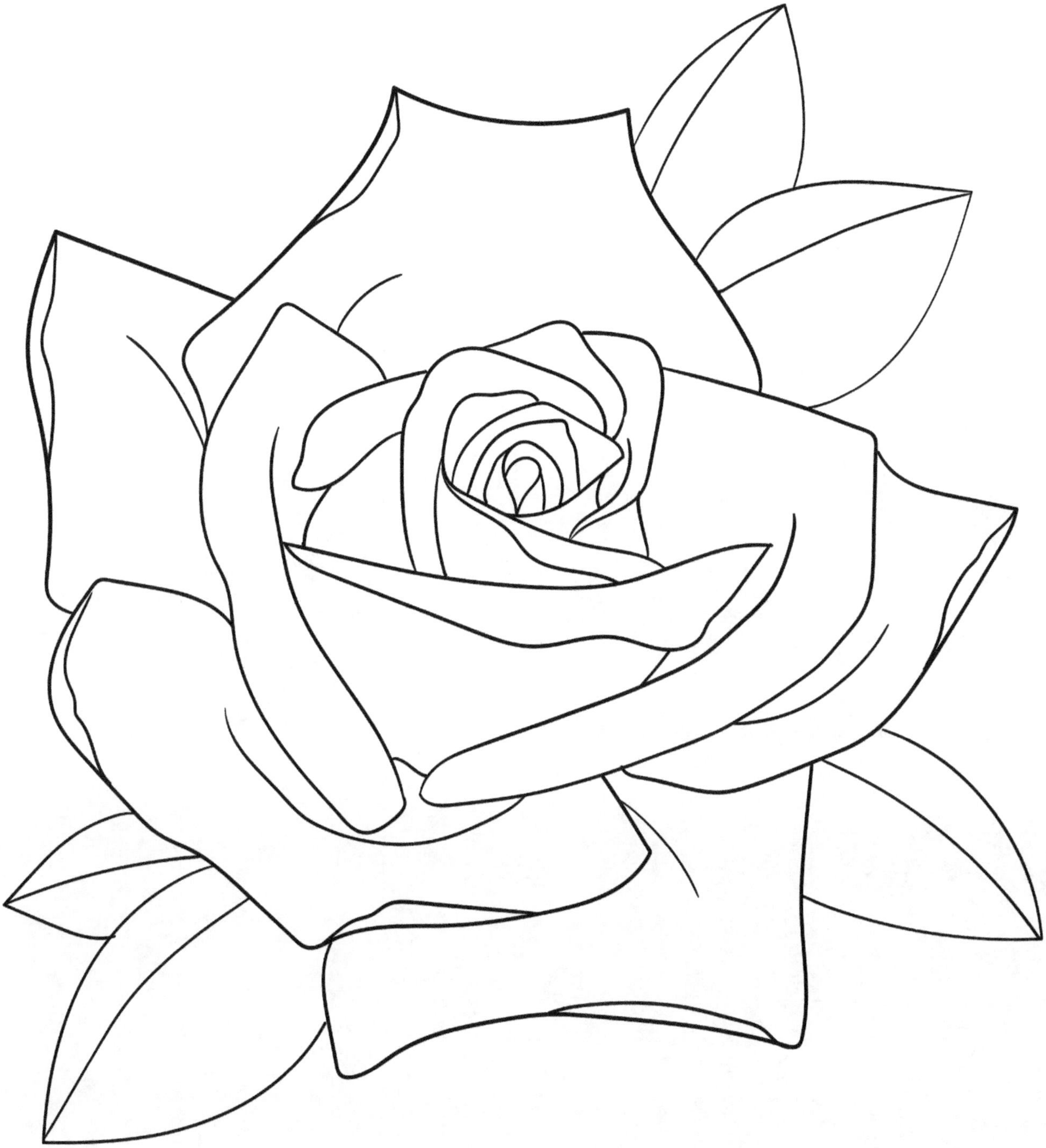

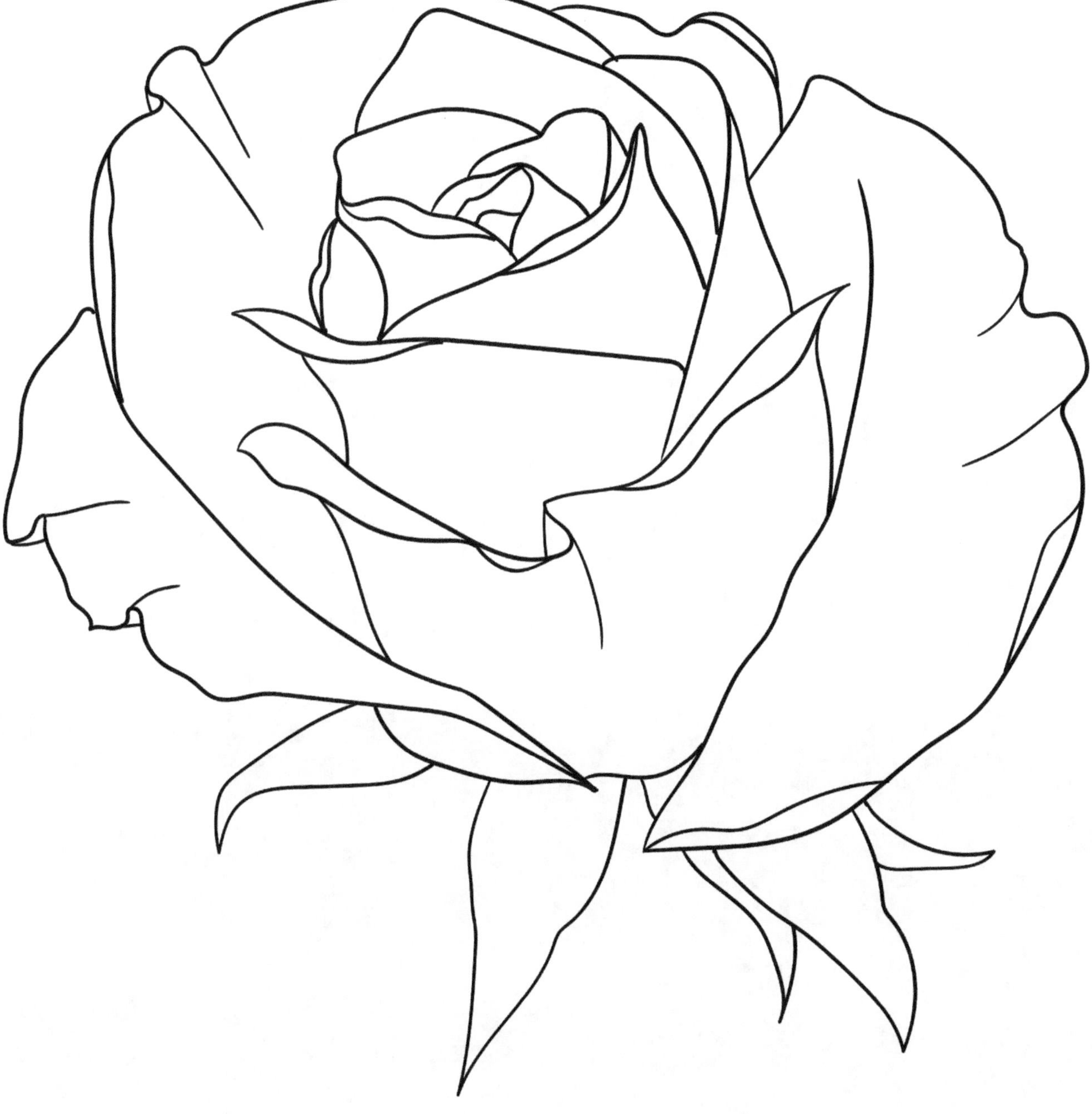

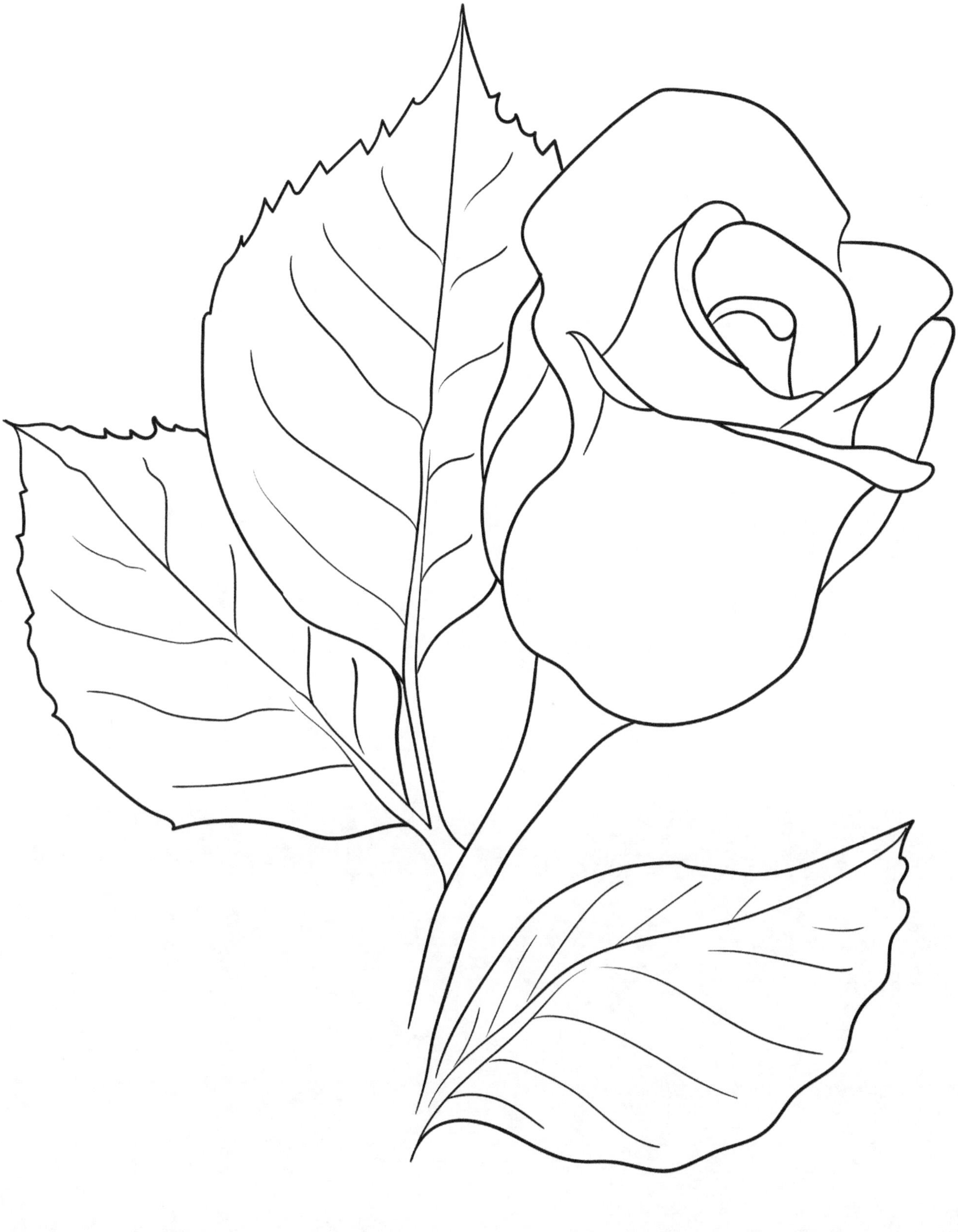

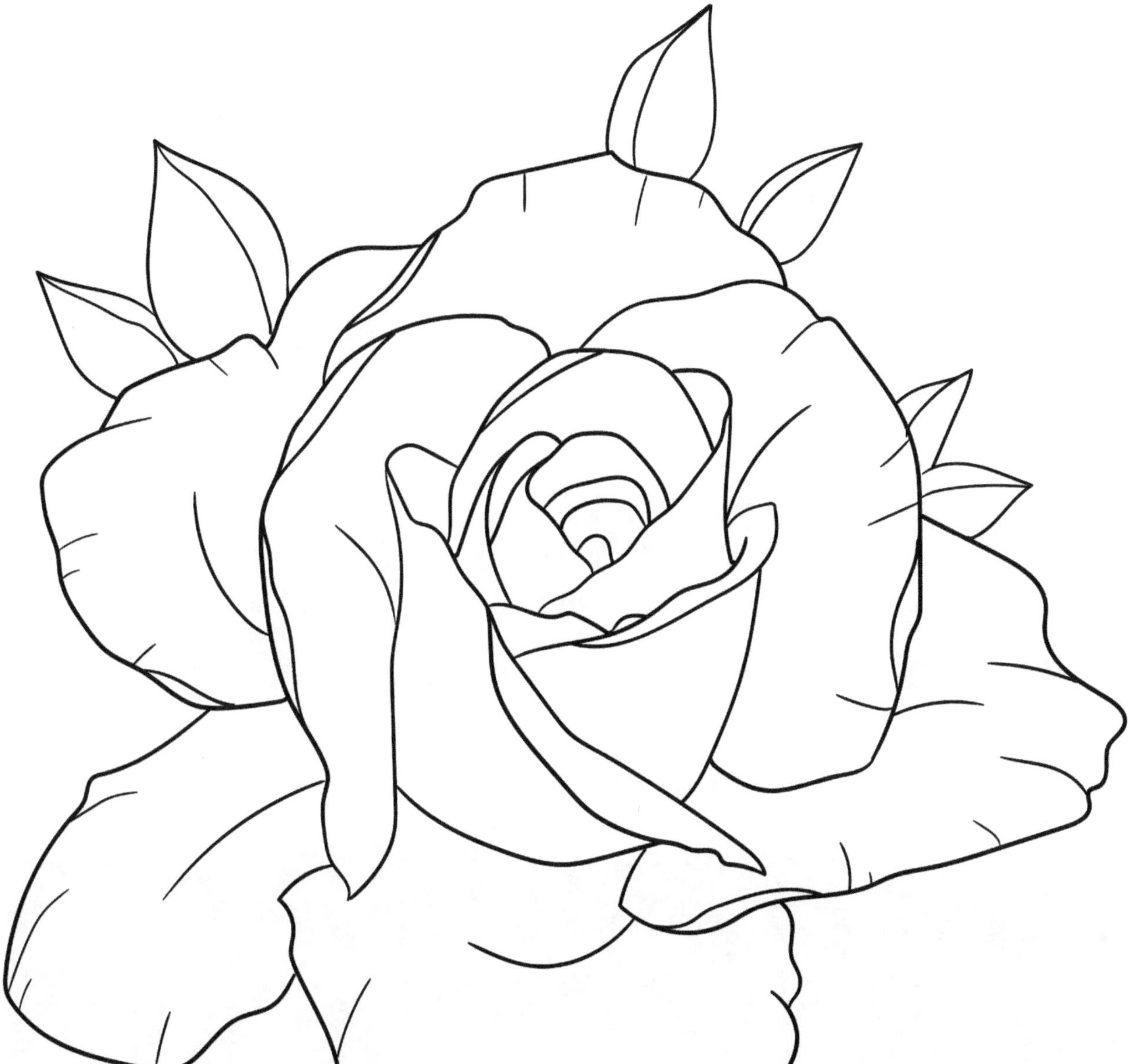

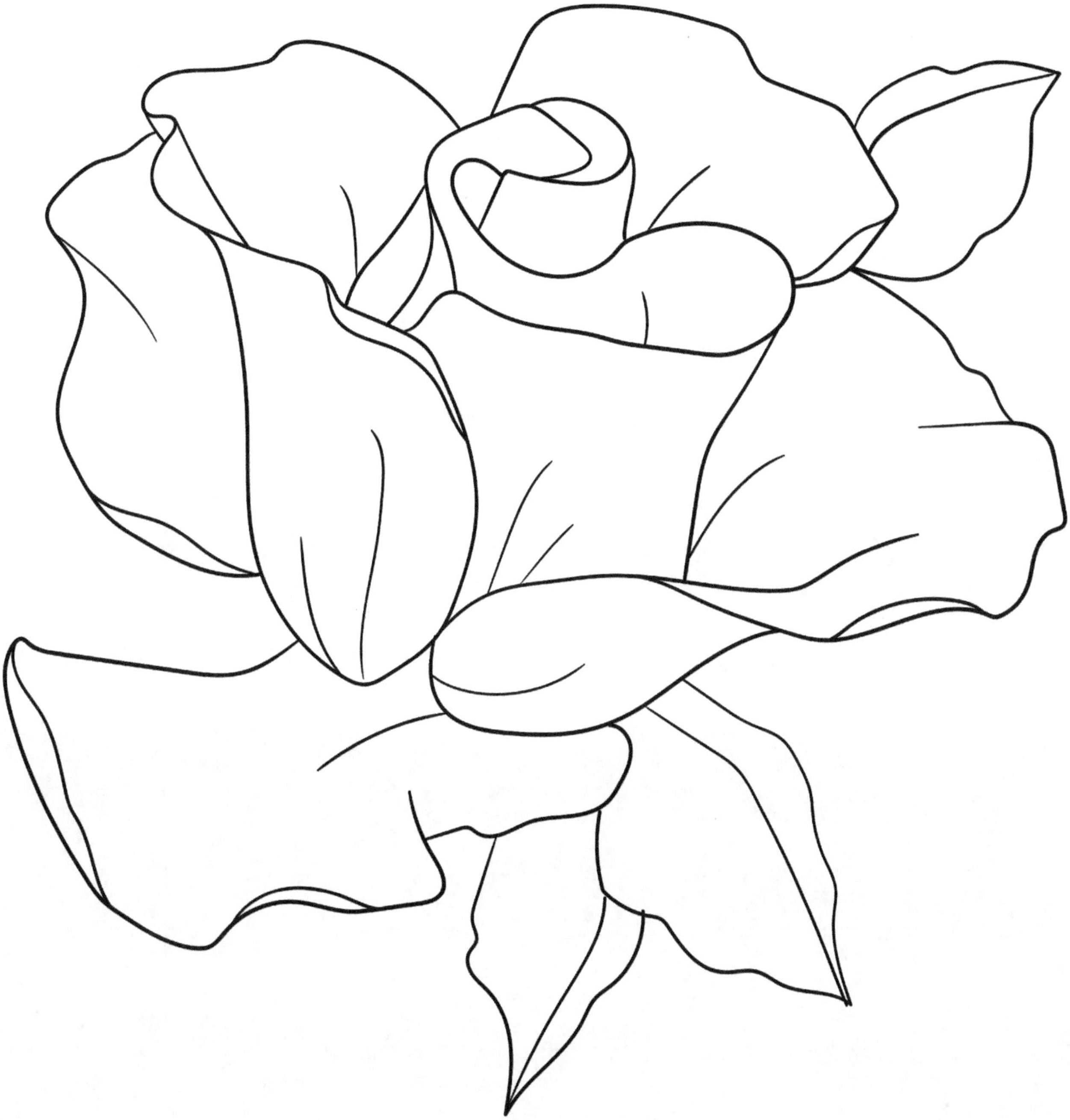

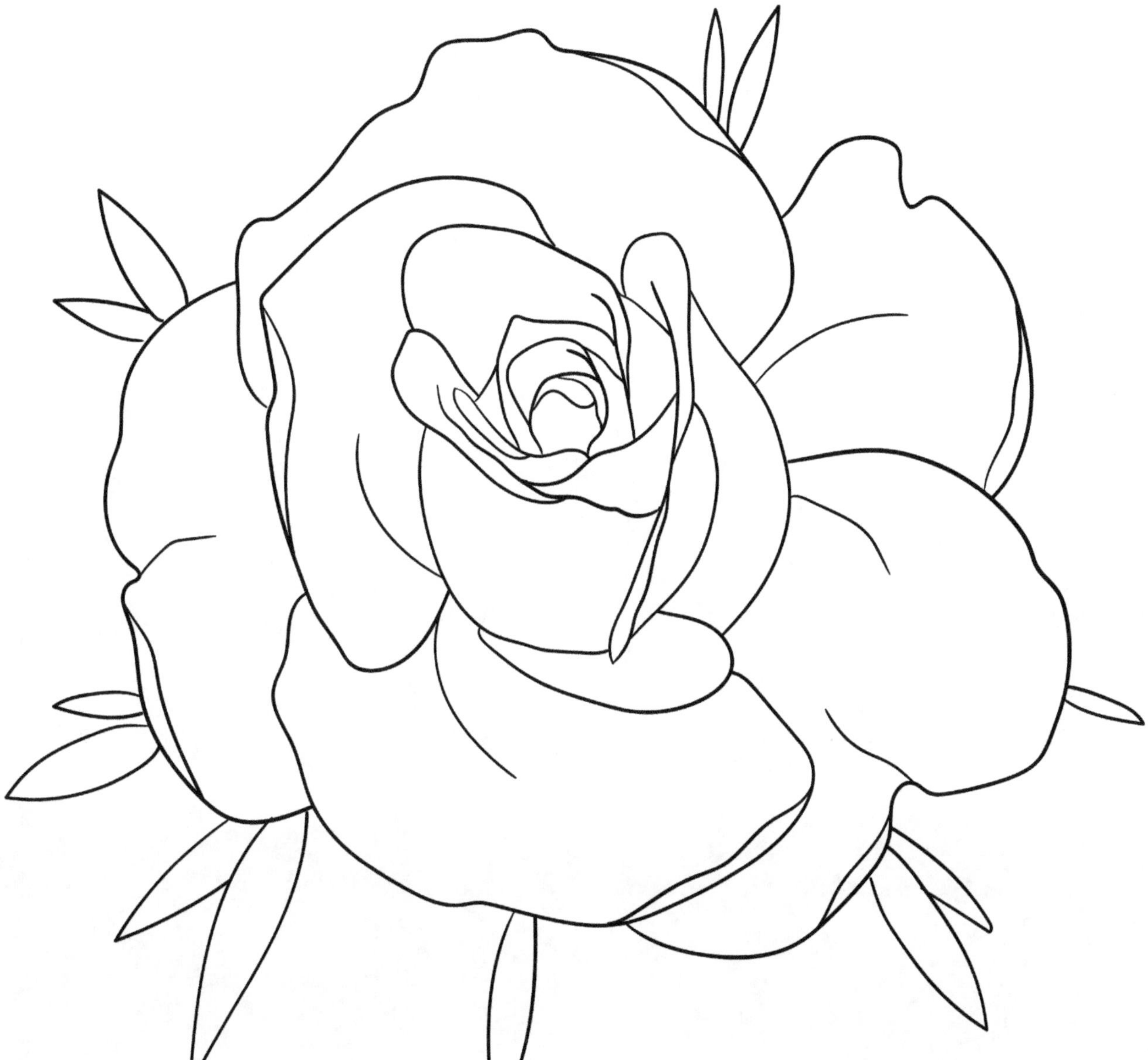

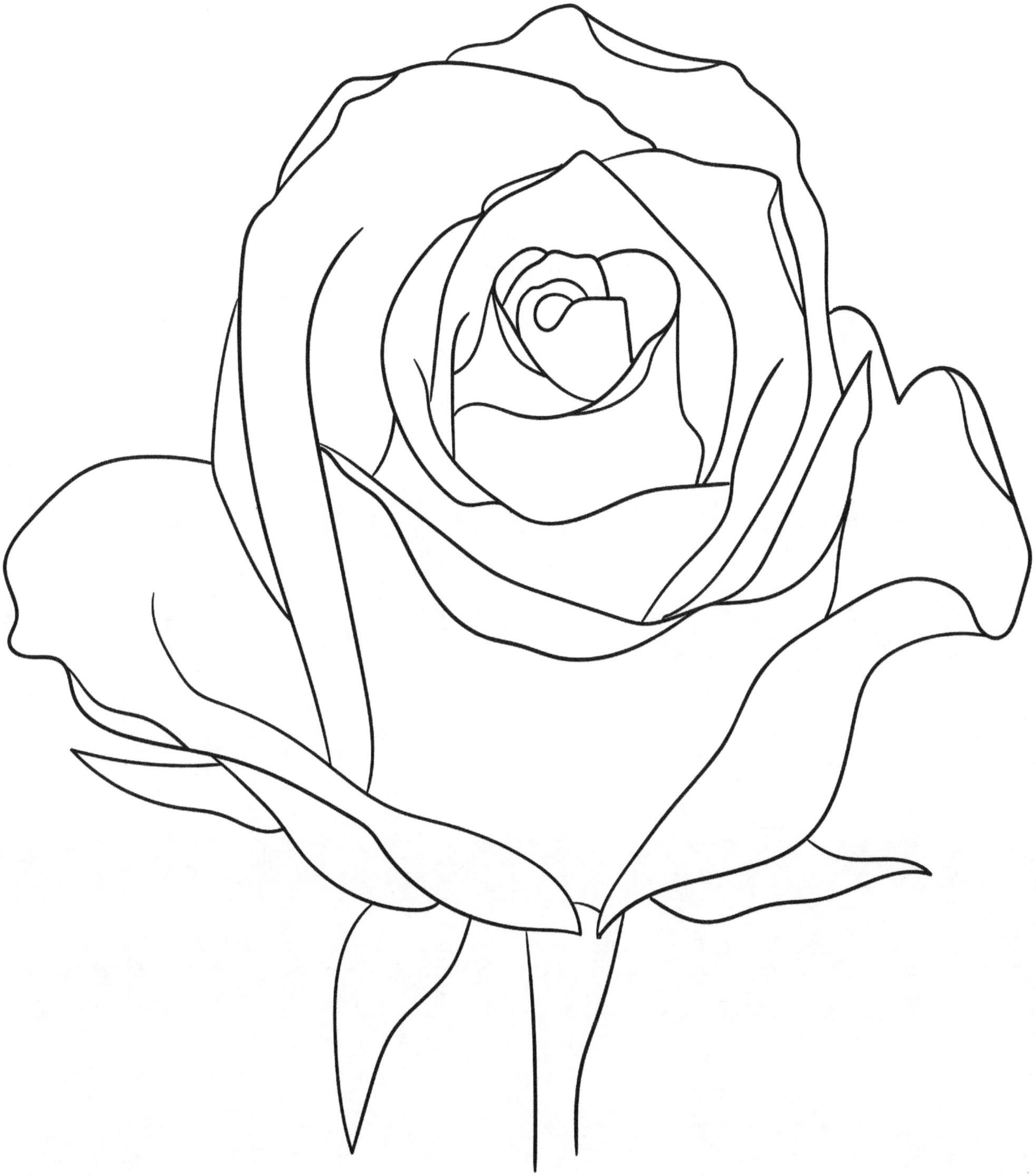

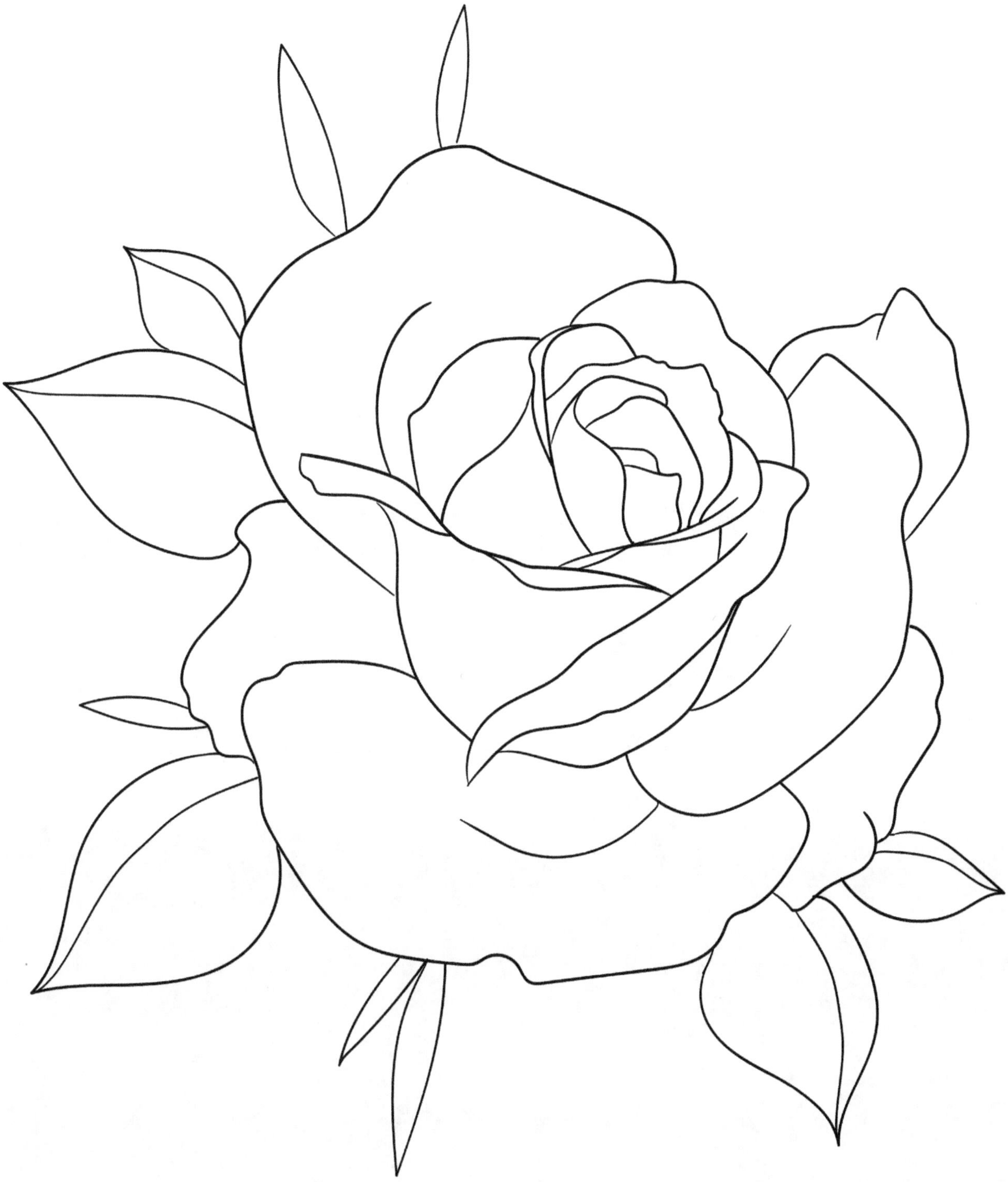

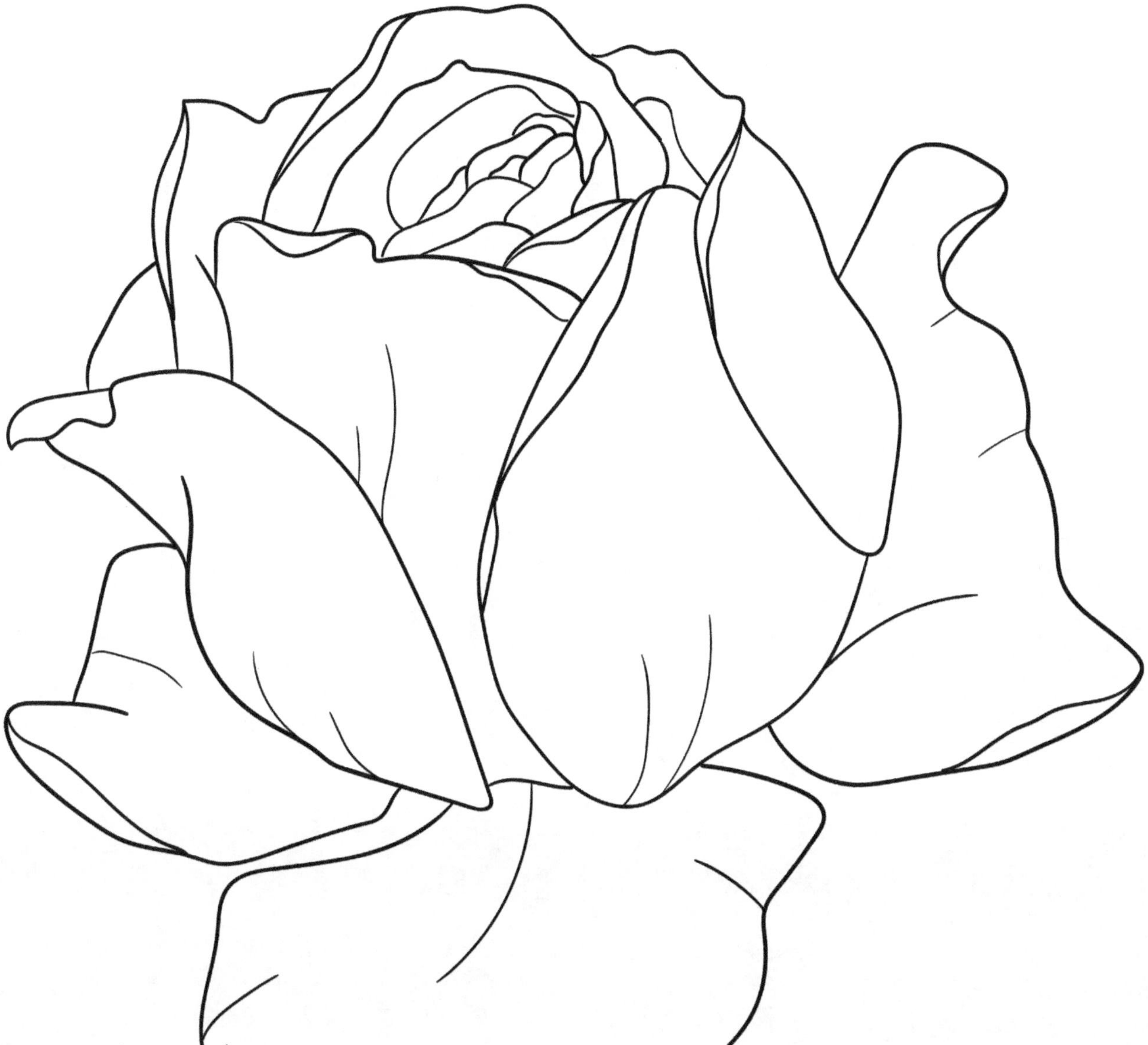

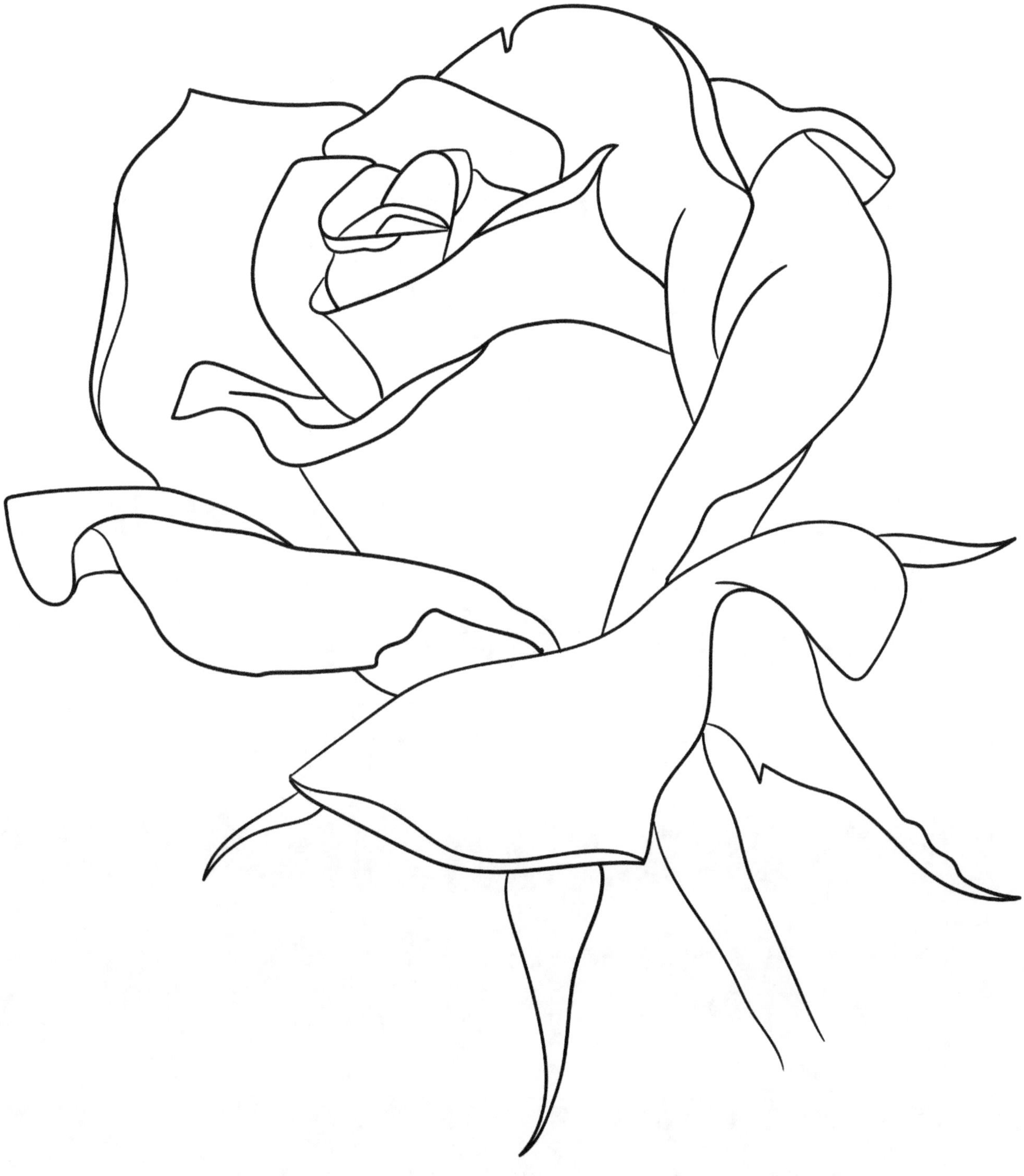

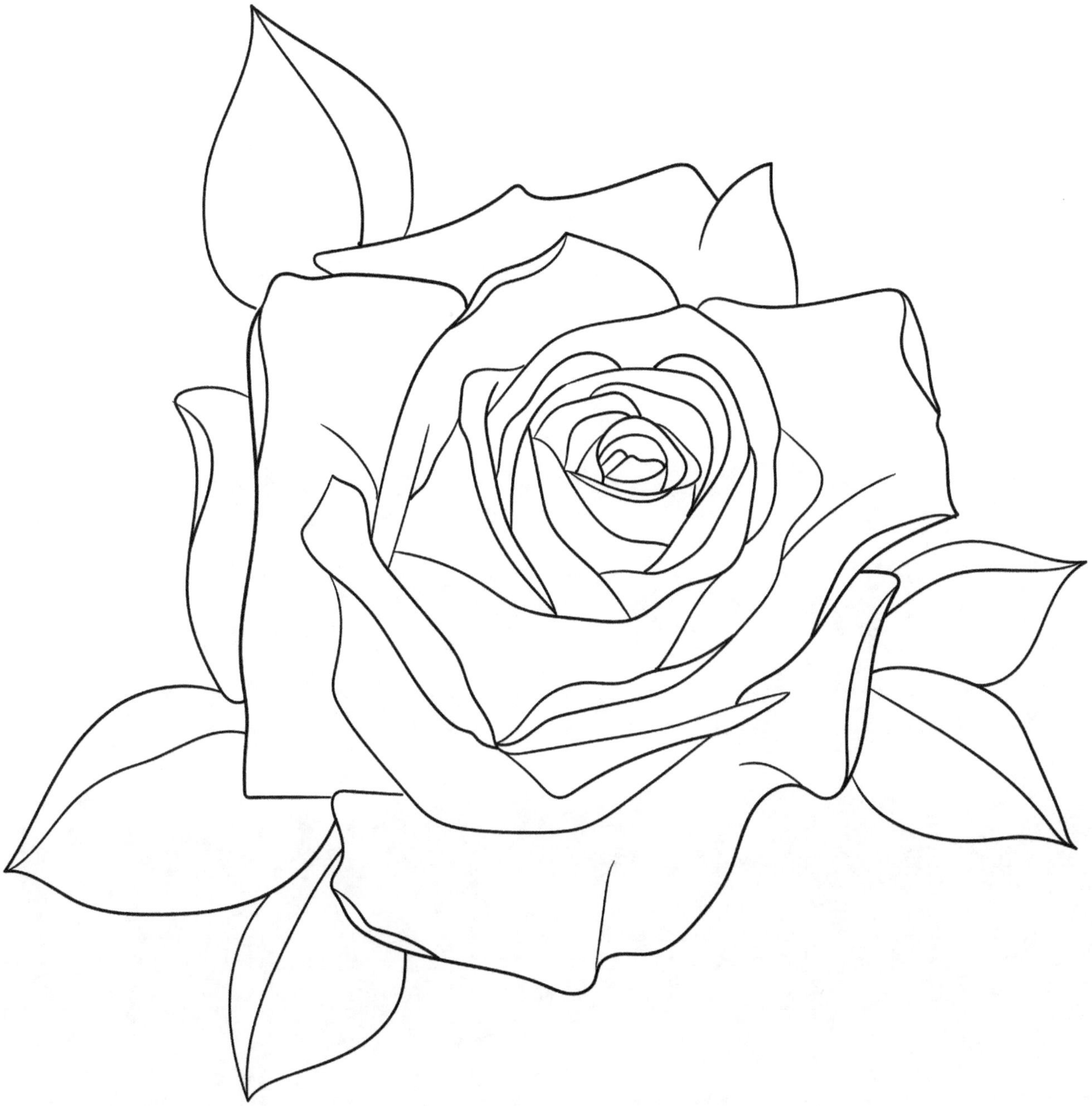

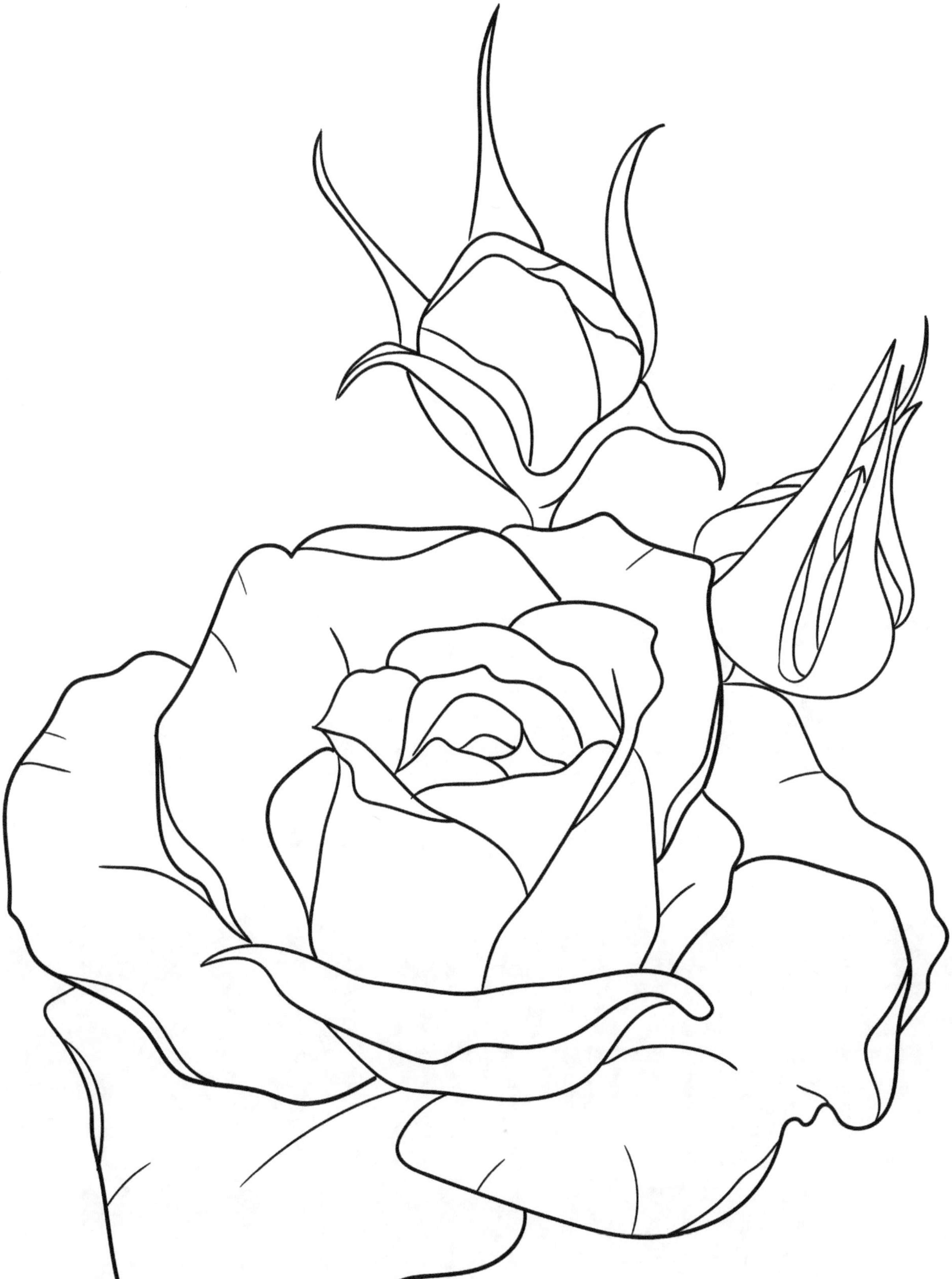

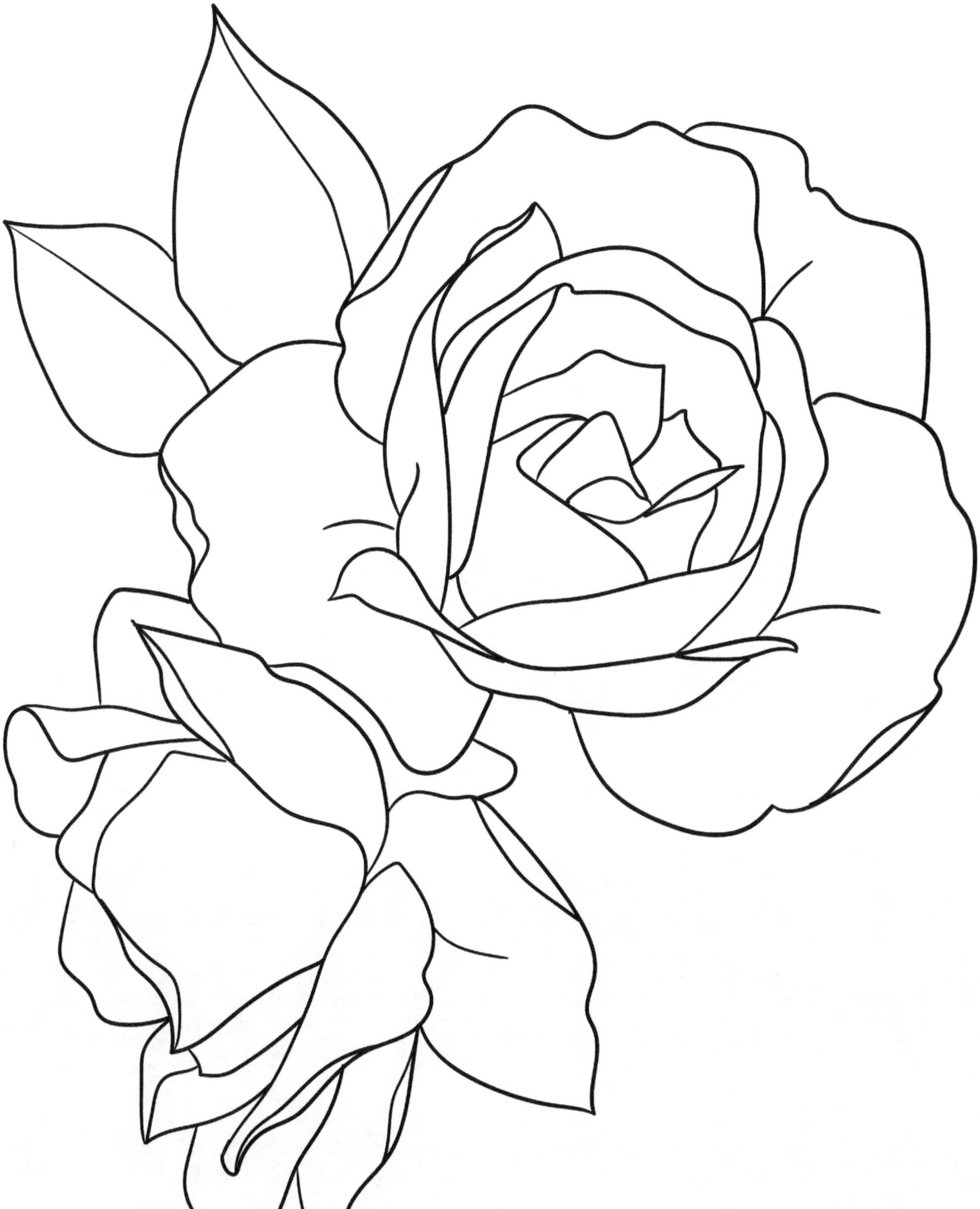

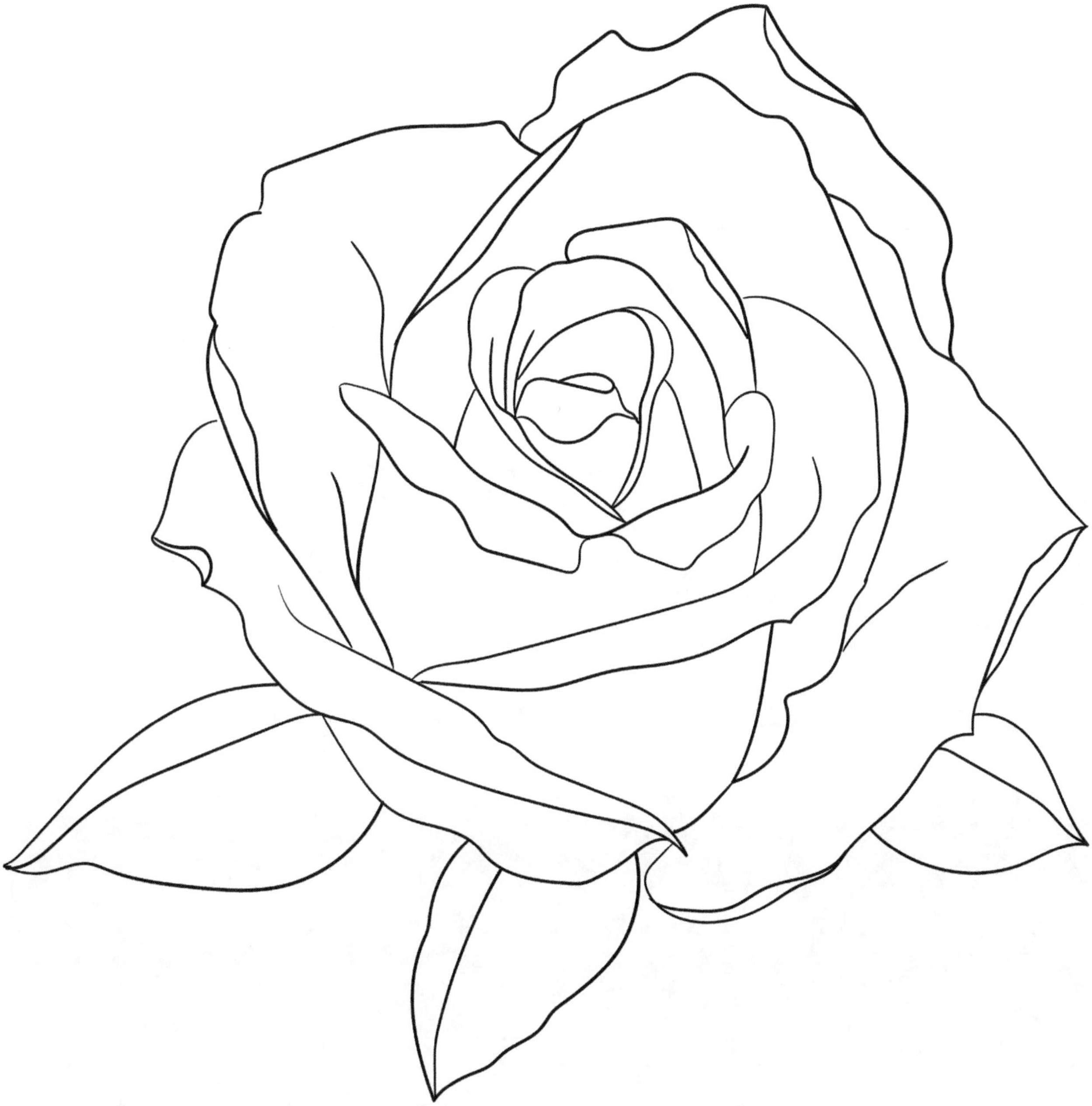

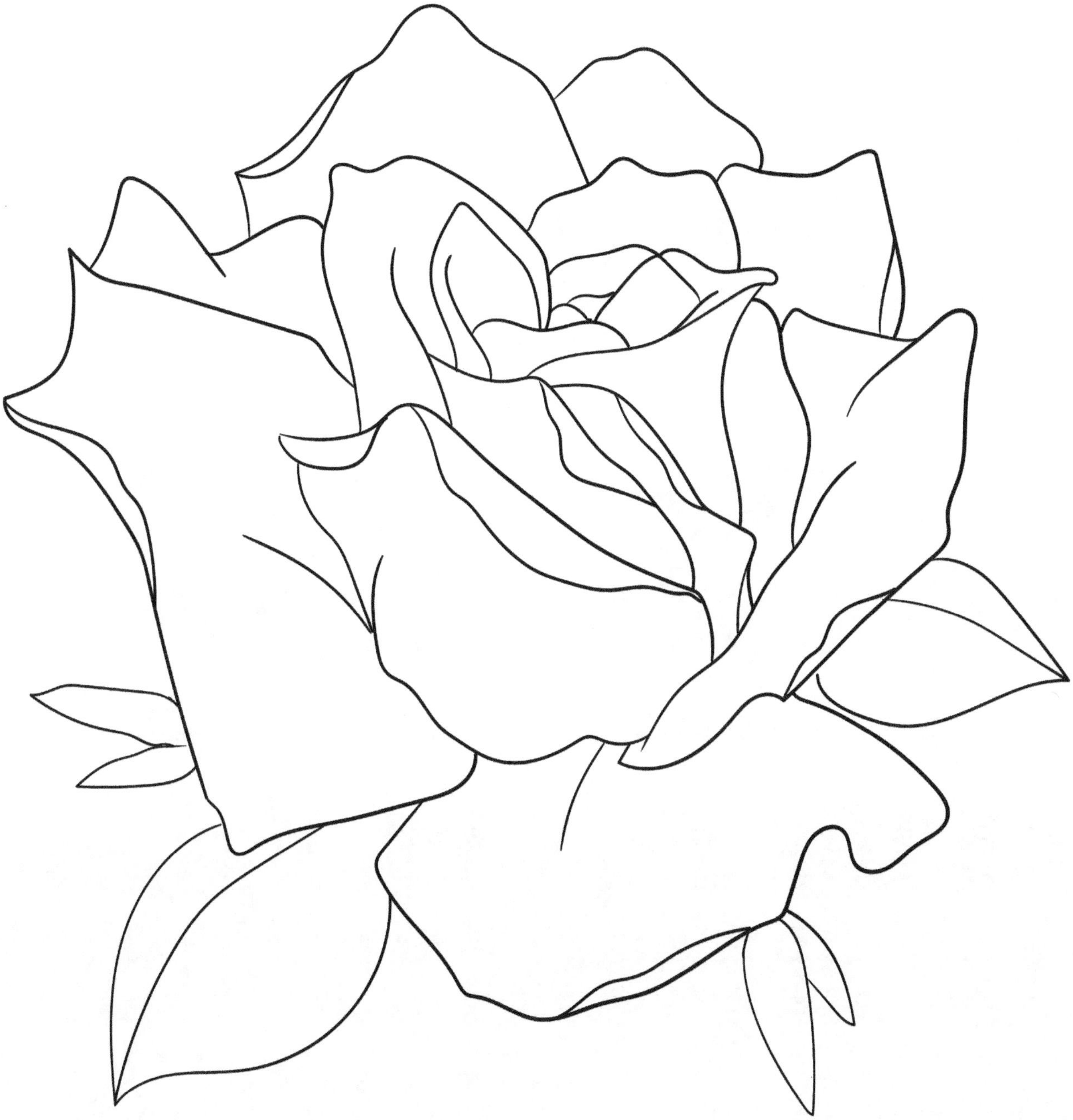

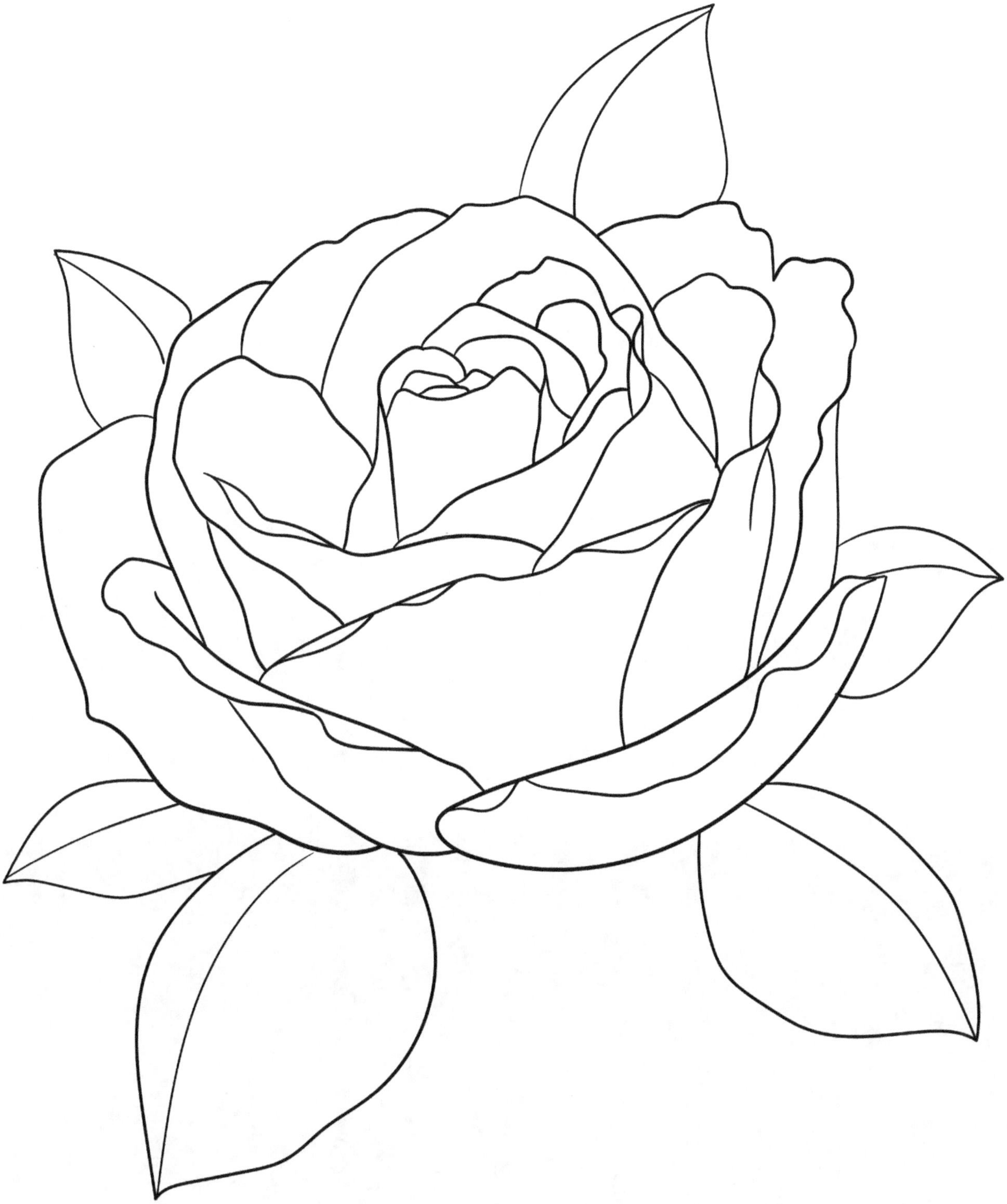

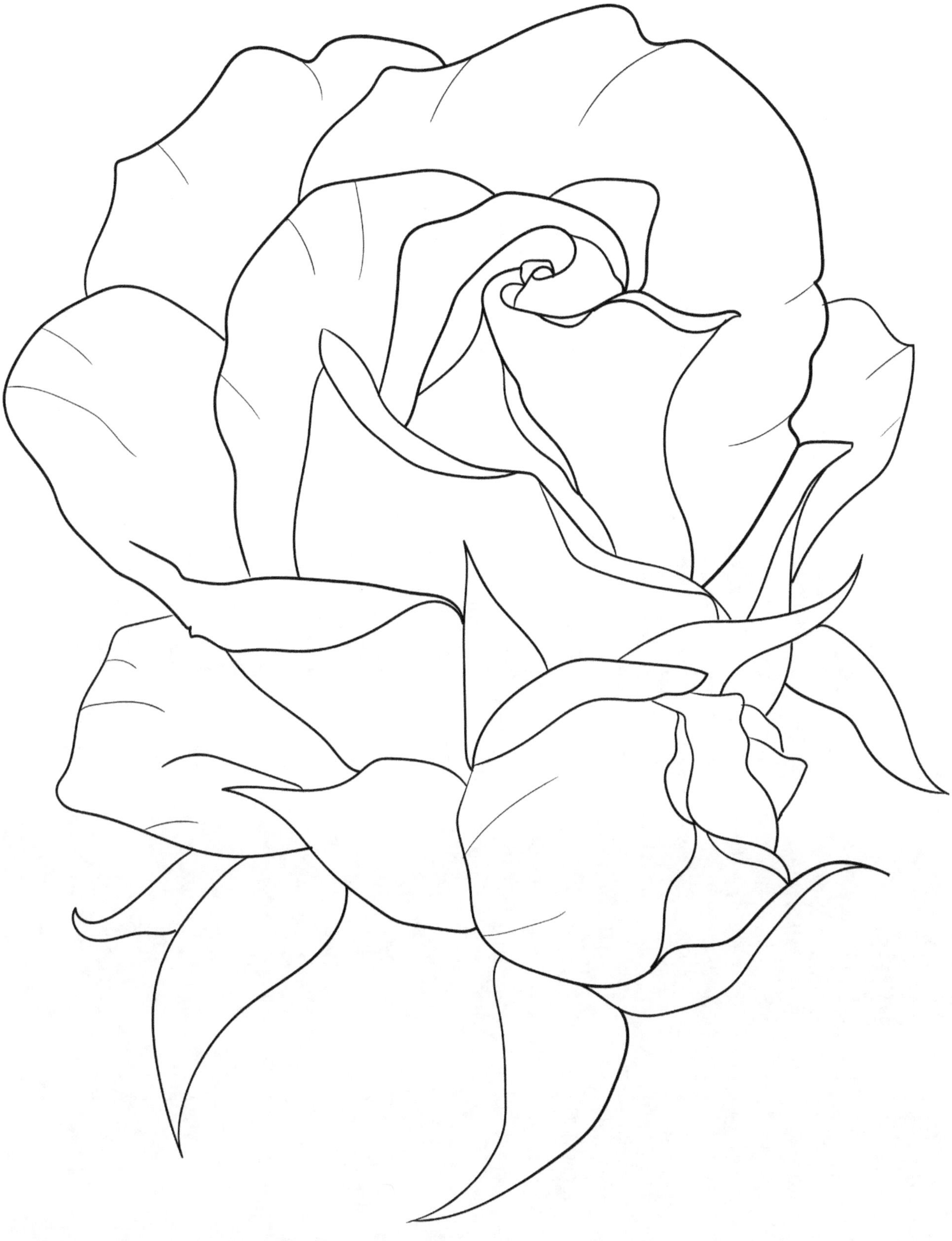

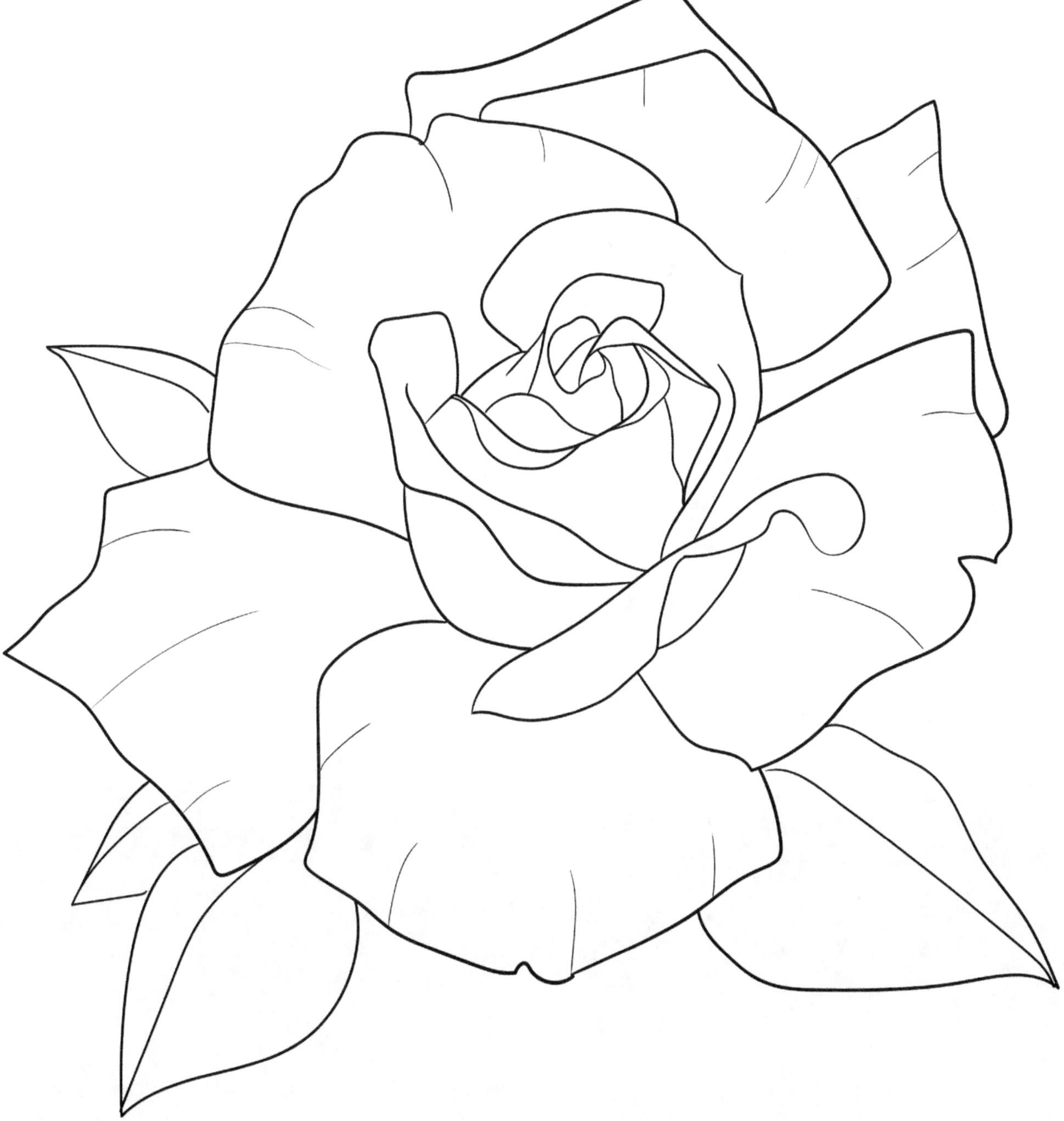

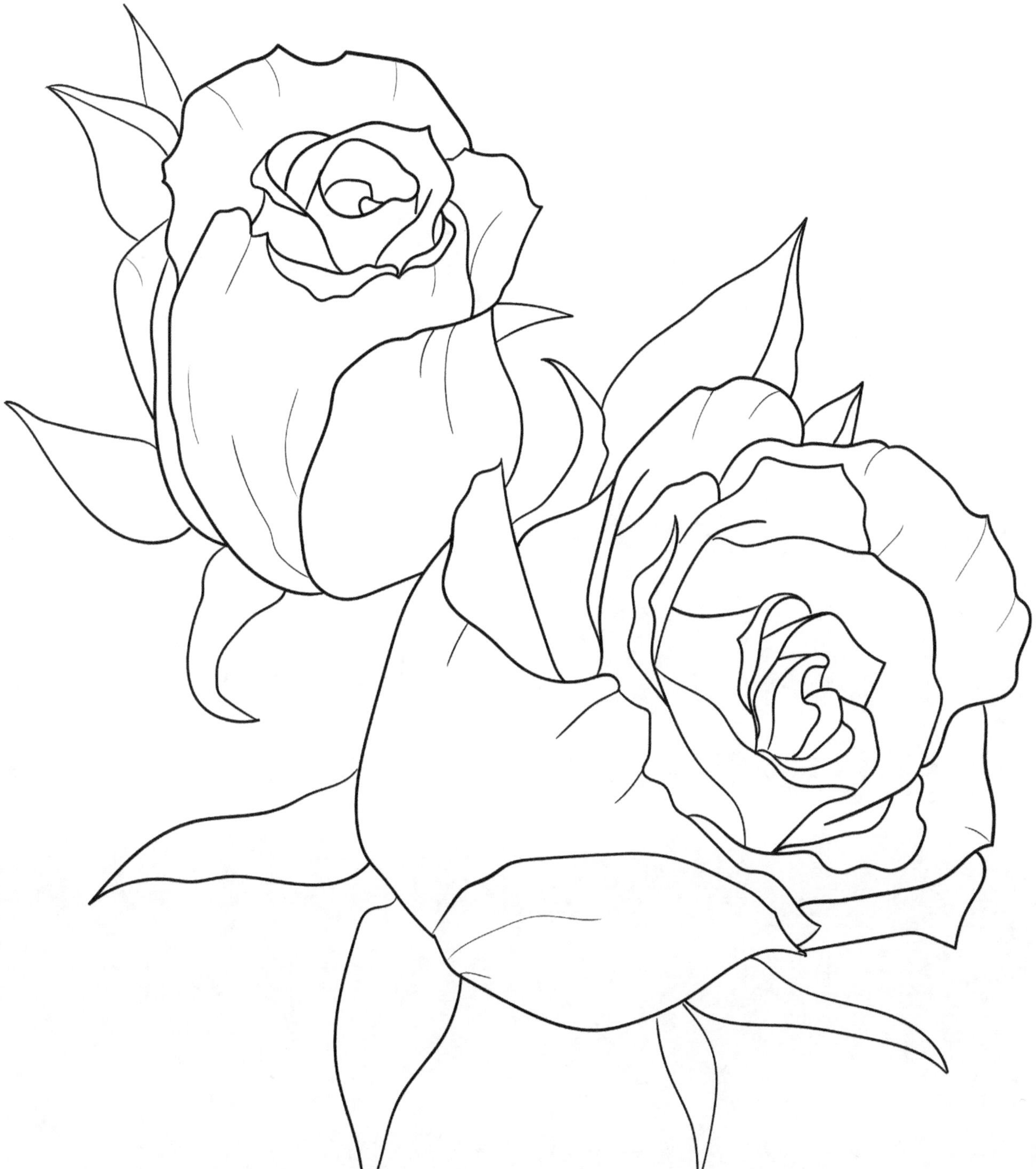

www.ingramcontent.com/pod-product-compliance
Lightning Source LLC
Chambersburg PA
CBHW080616180526
45168CB00007B/2941